Fern Brady

"Strong Female Character: The Fern Brady Story"

In the quaint town of Bathgate, Scotland, on the 26th of May, 1986, a girl named Fern Marie Brady embarked on a journey that would lead her through a tapestry of experiences, shaping her into a voice that resonates with humor, honesty, and a unique perspective on life. Fern's story is not just about comedy, but about self-discovery, resilience, and the power of embracing one's true self.

Chapter 1: Roots in Bathgate

Fern's early years were steeped in the cultural richness of her Irish descent, with family roots tracing back to County Donegal. Raised within the Catholic Church in Scotland, she experienced a childhood filled with the dual influences of her heritage and the Scottish environment. Her father, Paul, worked at Scania, managing the truck company's affairs, while her mother was a familiar face at the local Tesco. Despite their eventual divorce, Fern's parents laid the groundwork for her strong character and resilience.

Chapter 2: Education and Unexpected Paths

Fern's academic journey took her to St. Kentigern's Academy, Blackburn, where the seeds of her future were unknowingly sown. It was at the University of Edinburgh where Fern's path took an unexpected turn. As editor of The Student, a weekly newspaper, she honed her skills in writing and communication. But it was her job as a stripper to finance her studies that marked Fern's fearless approach to life – an approach that would later define her comedy.

Graduating with a Bachelor of Arts in Arabic and Islamic History, Fern initially ventured into journalism. However, the allure of comedy, a dream since 2006, beckoned.

Chapter 3: The Stand-Up Dream

Fern's foray into comedy began with an internship at Fest Magazine in 2009, where she was tasked with writing about a comedy critic trying stand-up. This experience was the catalyst that propelled her into the world of stand-up comedy. By May 2010, Fern Brady, the stand-up comedian, took to the stage, her wit and unique perspective captivating audiences.

Chapter 4: Rising Star

Her talent shone through in competitions such as "So You Think You're Funny" at the Edinburgh Festival Fringe and the Piccadilly Comedy Club new act competition. Television appearances on shows like 8 Out of 10 Cats and contributions to The Guardian showcased her growing influence in the comedy world.

Chapter 5: Embracing the Airwaves

In 2020, alongside Alison Spittle, Fern launched into the world of podcasting with "Wheel of Misfortune", a BBC podcast that echoed her distinct voice. That same year marked a significant turn in Fern's career as she co-presented "British as Folk" and launched her tour "Autistic Bikini Queen".

Chapter 6: A Revelation of Self

Fern's journey took a deeply personal turn in 2021 when she was diagnosed as being on the autism spectrum. This revelation brought clarity to her life, and she became an active voice in autism education. Her memoir, "Strong Female Character", published in 2023, not only won acclaim but also shed light on her personal experiences and her path to self-acceptance.

Chapter 7: Fern Brady Today

Today, Fern Brady stands as a symbol of strength, resilience, and authenticity. A bisexual woman who battled misdiagnoses before finding her truth, Fern's story is a testament to the power of embracing one's identity. Her humor, her voice, and her journey continue to inspire, making Fern Marie Brady a name synonymous with courage, laughter, and unwavering honesty.

"Fern Marie Brady: A Journey Through Laughter and Discovery"

Once upon a time in the rolling hills of West Lothian, Scotland, a girl named Fern Marie Brady was born into a world filled with the melodies of Irish folk songs and the hum of life in a small, close-knit community. Fern's early years in Bathgate were simple yet rich in cultural heritage, a tapestry of Irish and Scottish threads woven together by her family's history.

Her father, Paul, a man of practical skills managing Scania's truck business, and her mother, a familiar face at the local Tesco, provided a modest yet loving home. Though their paths would eventually part, they instilled in young Fern a sense of resilience and independence that would become the cornerstone of her journey.

As Fern grew, her spirited nature was evident. She found herself at St. Kentigern's Academy, where her sharp wit and keen observations often left her classmates in stitches. Little did they know, a star was quietly being born in their midst.

The turning point came when Fern moved to Edinburgh for university. Amidst the ancient cobblestone streets and the prestigious halls of the University of Edinburgh, she found herself drawn to the world of words and ideas. As the editor of The Student, she shaped the narratives that would define her generation. But in the shadows of the night, she moonlighted in a role far removed from the academic rigors – as a stripper. It was a daring choice, but one that spoke volumes of her fearlessness and determination to carve her own path.

With a degree in Arabic and Islamic History in hand, Fern set out to be a journalist. But fate had a different plan. Her stint at Fest Magazine in 2009, writing about a comedy critic trying stand-up, lit a spark within her. The thrill of making people laugh, the rush of standing on stage, it was intoxicating. By May 2010, Fern took the brave leap onto the stage, microphone in hand, ready to face the world with nothing but her wit.

The comedy circuit was abuzz with the name Fern Brady. She was the fresh voice everyone was talking about, her humor a blend of sharp insight and raw honesty. Competitions like "So You Think You're Funny" at the Edinburgh Festival Fringe saw her rise, her talent undeniable.

Television came calling, and Fern answered. Shows like 8 Out of 10 Cats and The News Quiz on BBC Radio 4 were just the beginning. Her words found a home in The Guardian, her opinions shaping discussions far beyond the comedy clubs.

In 2020, as the world faced uncertainties, Fern, alongside Alison Spittle, ventured into the world of podcasting with "Wheel of Misfortune." It was an instant hit, a testament to Fern's ever-evolving talent.

With a degree in Arabic and Islamic History in hand, Fern set out to be a journalist. But fate had a different plan. Her stint at Fest Magazine in 2009, writing about a comedy critic trying stand-up, lit a spark within her. The thrill of making people laugh, the rush of standing on stage, it was intoxicating. By May 2010, Fern took the brave leap onto the stage, microphone in hand, ready to face the world with nothing but her wit.

The comedy circuit was abuzz with the name Fern Brady. She was the fresh voice everyone was talking about, her humor a blend of sharp insight and raw honesty. Competitions like "So You Think You're Funny" at the Edinburgh Festival Fringe saw her rise, her talent undeniable.

Television came calling, and Fern answered. Shows like 8 Out of 10 Cats and The News Quiz on BBC Radio 4 were just the beginning. Her words found a home in The Guardian, her opinions shaping discussions far beyond the comedy clubs.

In 2020, as the world faced uncertainties, Fern, alongside Alison Spittle, ventured into the world of podcasting with "Wheel of Misfortune." It was an instant hit, a testament to Fern's ever-evolving talent.

In the heart of Scotland, where the laughter of Fern Brady once echoed through the halls of her school, her voice now resounded on a much grander stage. With every performance, every podcast episode, and each written word, she wove her experiences into a tapestry that resonated with authenticity and courage.

The year 2022 marked new horizons for Fern. The launch of her show "Autistic Bikini Queen" was not just another comedy tour; it was a celebration of her journey, a declaration of her identity, and an invitation to the world to laugh and learn along with her. The tour was a resounding success, with each venue filled with an audience eager to partake in Fern's unique blend of humor and heart.

But Fern's story was not just about standing in the spotlight. It was about shining that light on others as well. In late 2021, she co-presented "British as Folk" alongside fellow comedians Ivo Graham and Darren Harriott, exploring the diverse cultural landscape of Britain. Her insightful commentary and quick wit added depth and laughter to the travelogue, making it a hit with viewers.

As 2022 unfolded, Fern's journey took an exciting turn when she was confirmed as a contestant in the 14th series of "Taskmaster." Her participation in this beloved television show was a testament to her growing influence in the comedy world. Her unique brand of humor, coupled with her fearless spirit, made her a standout contestant, endearing her to a new wave of fans.

Fern's personal life, though less in the public eye, was equally rich and complex. Her bisexuality, a facet of her identity she openly embraced, was a part of her narrative that she shared with unapologetic honesty. Her earlier misdiagnosis with obsessive-compulsive disorder (OCD) and her later realization of being autistic were chapters in her life that spoke of missteps and misunderstandings in the journey towards self-discovery.

Her autism diagnosis, revealed in 2021, was a moment of profound introspection. Fern navigated this newfound understanding of herself with grace, using her platform to educate and advocate for others in the autism community. Her experiences, shared openly, became a source of comfort and inspiration for many who saw in her a kindred spirit.

As Fern's story continued to unfold, it was clear that her impact went far beyond the stages of comedy clubs and television screens. She became a voice for those who felt unseen, a champion for authenticity in a world often masked by pretense. Her memoir "Strong Female Character" was not just a recounting of her life; it was a manifesto of resilience, a call to embrace one's truth, no matter how daunting that truth might be.

Fern's journey, a blend of laughter and self-discovery, continued to unfold with each passing day. Her story was a reminder that life, in all its complexity and unpredictability, is a canvas waiting to be painted with our unique colors. Fern Marie Brady, with her indomitable spirit and unwavering honesty, painted her canvas with bold strokes, inspiring others to pick up their brushes and join in the beautiful, chaotic art of living.

As Fern Marie Brady's journey unfolded, it became clear that her story was more than just a tale of personal triumph; it was a beacon of hope and inspiration for others navigating their own complex paths.

In 2024, Fern's influence continued to grow. Her voice, once confined to the comedy clubs of Scotland, now reached global audiences. Through her podcast, "Wheel of Misfortune," she connected with listeners from all walks of life, sharing stories of misadventures and mishaps with humor and humanity. The podcast became a sanctuary of laughter and empathy, where listeners found solace in Fern's candid discussions about life's unpredictable turns.

Fern's role in "Taskmaster" had also elevated her to new heights of popularity. Her clever strategies and infectious humor on the show not only entertained but also highlighted her unique perspective on life's challenges. Fans appreciated her authenticity, and she became a role model for embracing one's quirks and differences.

Beyond the entertainment world, Fern's advocacy for autism awareness grew more potent. She spoke at conferences and participated in events, using her platform to shed light on the nuances of living with autism. Her candid discussions about her experiences provided invaluable insights, helping to dismantle stereotypes and promote a deeper understanding of the autistic community.

In her personal life, Fern's journey was equally transformative. Her open discussions about her bisexuality and mental health challenges broke down barriers and fostered a culture of openness and acceptance. She became a symbol of strength for the LGBTQ+ community and those battling mental health issues, proving that one's trials could become their greatest strengths.

Her memoir, "Strong Female Character," continued to touch hearts. Readers found in its pages not just the story of a comedian finding her voice but also a tale of personal metamorphosis. The memoir's success led to numerous speaking engagements, where Fern shared her insights on resilience, self-acceptance, and the power of storytelling.

As Fern navigated the twists and turns of her career and personal life, she remained grounded in her roots. She often reminisced about her days in Bathgate, the values instilled by her parents, and the rich cultural tapestry of her Irish and Scottish heritage. These reflections brought a depth to her comedy and writings, infusing them with a relatable and heartfelt authenticity.

Fern's impact extended beyond her immediate sphere as she inspired a new generation of comedians, writers, and activists. She showed that with courage, humor, and a willingness to be vulnerable, one could not only face their challenges but also turn them into a source of empowerment.

Fern Marie Brady's story was a testament to the power of embracing one's true self, the beauty of human imperfection, and the transformative power of laughter. As she continued to write her story, one filled with both joy and challenges, Fern became more than just a comedian or a writer; she became a symbol of hope and resilience, a beacon shining brightly in the lives of those who found pieces of their own stories intertwined with hers.

As the year 2024 progressed, Fern Marie Brady's influence and impact continued to ripple across various spheres, transcending the bounds of comedy and touching the lives of many in profound ways.

In this year, Fern embarked on a new project that combined her comedic talents with her advocacy work. She launched a series of workshops aimed at young adults on the autism spectrum, where she used humor as a tool for self-expression and communication. These workshops, held in various cities, became a sanctuary for many who struggled with social interactions, offering them a space to explore their identities and express themselves freely. Fern's ability to connect with her audience, drawing from her own experiences, made these sessions not only educational but deeply empowering.

Her influence in the realm of mental health and autism awareness grew exponentially. Fern was invited to collaborate with researchers and psychologists, providing insights from her lived experiences to help shape more inclusive and effective mental health services. Her contributions were recognized by several mental health organizations, and she was honored with awards that acknowledged her work in destigmatizing mental health issues and autism.

On the personal front, Fern's journey of self-discovery and acceptance continued to evolve. She began writing her second book, delving deeper into the nuances of her identity and experiences. This new project promised to be an even more introspective work, exploring themes of love, belonging, and the continual process of self-realization. Her fans eagerly awaited this new chapter, anticipating a work that would once again connect deeply with their own experiences.

Fern's presence on social media also became a source of inspiration and solidarity. Her honest and often humorous posts about daily life, the challenges of being on the autism spectrum, and the joys and trials of her career resonated with a wide audience. She cultivated a community where openness and vulnerability were not just accepted but celebrated.

In comedy, Fern continued to push boundaries. She returned to the Edinburgh Fringe Festival, the place where her comedy career had taken flight, with a show that was hailed as her best yet. This new act was a blend of poignant storytelling and razor-sharp wit, showcasing her growth as a comedian and as an individual. Critics and audiences alike praised her for her ability to tackle complex subjects with humor and sensitivity.

Despite her growing fame, Fern remained grounded. She often returned to Bathgate, where her journey began, to reconnect with her roots and to find the grounding and inspiration for her work. These visits were a reminder of the unassuming beginnings of her story, a story that continued to unfold with each passing day.

As the years went by, Fern Marie Brady's legacy grew not just as a comedian, but as a voice of change, an advocate for mental health and autism awareness, and a beacon of hope for many. Her life, a vivid tapestry of challenges, triumphs, and unending growth, stood as a testament to the power of resilience, the beauty of authenticity, and the transformative power of embracing one's unique journey. Her story continued, each chapter more inspiring than the last, encouraging everyone who came across it to laugh, learn, and live with an open heart.

In the latter part of 2024, Fern Brady's story took a new, exciting turn as she ventured into the world of television production. Drawing from her vast experiences, she began working on a semi-autobiographical comedy series. The show, which she wrote and starred in, was a witty and poignant exploration of the life of a bisexual, autistic woman navigating the complexities of modern life. This project was not just a personal triumph for Fern but also a groundbreaking moment for representation on television. Her character, imbued with Fern's own experiences and insights, brought a fresh, authentic perspective to the screen, resonating with audiences far and wide.

Meanwhile, Fern's advocacy efforts continued to gain momentum. Her workshops for autistic individuals expanded internationally, reaching audiences in the United States and Europe. She collaborated with autism charities to create resources and support networks, further solidifying her role as a key figure in the autism community. Her efforts were recognized globally, and she was invited to speak at the United Nations on World Autism Awareness Day, where she delivered a powerful speech about inclusion, diversity, and the importance of understanding and embracing neurodiversity.

Back in Scotland, Fern remained deeply connected to her roots. She organized a comedy festival in her hometown of Bathgate, featuring local and national comedians. The festival was not just a celebration of comedy but also a way for Fern to give back to the community that had nurtured her. The event was a huge success, blending humor with charity, as proceeds went towards mental health and autism support groups.

Fern's second book, a deeper dive into her life journey, was released to critical acclaim. Titled "Beyond the Laughter," the book was a more intimate portrayal of her struggles, victories, and the lessons learned along the way. Readers found her honesty refreshing and her insights invaluable, further cementing her status as a prominent voice in discussions about mental health and self-acceptance.

On the personal front, Fern's life was a tapestry of rich experiences and relationships. She became a mentor to young comedians, particularly those from marginalized communities, offering guidance and support. Her personal life, though she kept it private, was known to be filled with love and laughter, shared with close friends and family who kept her grounded.

As Fern looked to the future, she envisioned new ways to blend her comedy with her advocacy. Her goal was not just to entertain but to enlighten, to not only make people laugh but also make them think. Her journey was a beacon of hope, showing that it was possible to turn one's struggles into strengths, to use one's voice to effect change, and to live a life that was as deeply meaningful as it was joyfully humorous.

Fern Marie Brady's story, ever-evolving, remained a source of inspiration. It was a reminder that life, in all its unpredictability and complexity, could be a beautiful journey of self-discovery, growth, and laughter. Through her comedy, writing, and activism, Fern continued to touch lives, leaving an indelible mark on the world, one laugh, one lesson, one heart at a time.

As 2025 dawned, Fern Brady's influence and impact continued to flourish in new and unexpected ways. Her television series, now in its second season, had become a cultural touchstone, celebrated for its unflinching honesty and humor. It was more than entertainment; it was a platform that sparked conversations about neurodiversity, sexuality, and the myriad ways of being human. The show won several awards, but for Fern, the real reward was the messages from viewers who saw their experiences reflected on screen for the first time.

This period also saw Fern venturing into the world of filmmaking. She began developing a documentary that sought to explore the lives of autistic individuals from different cultures around the world. Her aim was to shed light on the diverse experiences within the autism spectrum, challenging stereotypes and broadening understanding. The project was a labor of love, combining her skills as a journalist, her flair for storytelling, and her personal insights.

Fern's influence in the realm of mental health advocacy also continued to expand. She was instrumental in launching a series of online platforms that offered support and resources for people with autism and their families. These platforms also served as communities where people could share experiences and support each other, much like Fern had done through her comedy and public speaking.

In Scotland, Fern's comedy festival in Bathgate had grown, becoming an annual event that attracted talent from across the globe. It was more than just a festival; it was a celebration of diversity, inclusivity, and the power of laughter to bring people together. Fern used this platform to support up-and-coming comedians, particularly those from underrepresented backgrounds, giving them a stage to showcase their talents.

Her personal life, always guarded from the public eye, remained a source of stability and joy. She often spoke of the importance of maintaining a balance, of having a sanctuary away from the spotlight. Fern found solace in nature, in quiet moments spent in the Scottish countryside, which provided her with inspiration and a sense of peace.

As she looked to the future, Fern had numerous projects in the pipeline. She was working on a new book, a collection of essays on comedy, life, and the intersections of her identity. She was also planning a global tour, bringing her unique brand of comedy and storytelling to audiences around the world.

Fern Marie Brady had become more than a comedian or an advocate; she was a symbol of resilience, a voice for the underrepresented, and a testament to the power of using one's talents and experiences to make a difference. Her journey continued to inspire, to challenge, and to bring laughter and insight to people across the world. In her story, many found the courage to embrace their own truths, to celebrate their differences, and to understand that in the tapestry of human experience, every thread, no matter how unique, was essential and beautiful.

As Fern Brady's global tour commenced in 2026, her influence as a comedian and advocate reached new heights. She traveled across continents, her shows selling out in major cities worldwide. Each performance was more than just a night of laughter; it was an experience that brought together diverse audiences to celebrate the universality of humor and the unique perspectives Fern offered.

The tour, aptly named "Laughing Through the Spectrum," was a vibrant blend of comedy, storytelling, and honest discourse about life on the autism spectrum. Fern's ability to connect with her audience, to make them laugh and think simultaneously, was her signature. Her shows were not just entertaining; they were eye-opening experiences that challenged perceptions and fostered a deeper understanding of neurodiversity.

Back in Scotland, Fern's documentary on autism around the world premiered to critical acclaim. Titled "Unseen Spectrums," it was a poignant, eye-opening journey into the lives of autistic individuals from different cultures, showcasing their challenges, triumphs, and the diverse ways they navigated a world not always accommodating of their needs. The documentary was praised for its empathy, insight, and the respectful portrayal of its subjects. It became a valuable resource in

, promoting greater awareness and understanding of autism.

Fern's documentary success fueled further projects. She began working on a series of short films, each telling the story of an individual living with autism, capturing their daily lives, aspirations, and the unique ways they experienced the world. These films were not just educational tools; they were works of art, celebrating the beauty and diversity of the human experience. They resonated with viewers, both within the autism community and beyond, fostering a sense of connection and empathy.

In her personal life, Fern remained grounded despite her growing fame. She often returned to Bathgate, where she found comfort in the familiarity of her childhood surroundings. She used these visits to reconnect with her roots and to draw inspiration for her work. Fern also devoted time to mentor young comedians and writers, particularly those from underrepresented communities, helping to nurture the next generation of talent.

In 2027, Fern released her third book, a collection of humorous yet insightful essays titled "Life on the Laugh Spectrum." The book was a bestseller, praised for its witty and poignant reflections on life, identity, and the power of humor. In these essays, Fern shared her journey with greater depth, revealing the challenges she faced and the lessons she learned along the way. Readers found comfort and inspiration in her words, seeing parts of their own journeys reflected in hers.

Fern's advocacy work continued to evolve. She launched an initiative to create sensory-friendly comedy shows, making live comedy more accessible to individuals with sensory sensitivities. These shows, with adjusted lighting and sound, relaxed rules about movement and noise, and designated quiet areas, were a hit, making the joy of live comedy available to a wider audience.

As Fern's reputation grew, she was invited to speak at global forums and conferences, sharing her insights on comedy, neurodiversity, and mental health. She became a sought-after voice in these fields, respected for her unique perspective and her ability to articulate complex ideas with humor and clarity.

Despite her busy schedule, Fern maintained a balance in her life, prioritizing her well-being and personal relationships. She found solace in writing, nature, and the close bonds she shared with her friends and family. These elements of her life provided her with the strength and inspiration to continue her journey.

As the years passed, Fern Marie Brady's legacy continued to grow. She was not just a comedian; she was a beacon of hope, a voice for those often unheard, and a shining example of how one's unique experiences can be transformed into a powerful force for change and understanding. Her story, a tapestry of laughter, struggle, and triumph, continued to inspire and resonate with people around the world, reminding everyone that in the vast spectrum of humanity, every color, every shade, is essential and beautiful.

As Fern Brady entered the next chapter of her career, her role as an advocate and artist took on new dimensions. In 2028, she embarked on a collaborative project with other artists and advocates, creating an international arts festival dedicated to neurodiversity. The festival, named "Spectrum of Expression," showcased films, visual arts, music, and literature created by neurodiverse artists from around the world. It was a celebration of creativity, a platform for voices often marginalized, and a powerful statement about the richness neurodiversity brings to the arts. Fern's involvement in the festival not only highlighted her commitment to inclusion but also her belief in the transformative power of art.

Meanwhile, Fern's personal journey of self-discovery and advocacy was captured in a documentary film. This deeply personal and introspective film offered a behind-the-scenes look at her life, her creative process, and her advocacy work. Audiences were given an intimate glimpse into the challenges and triumphs she faced, both as a public figure and in her private life. The documentary, titled "In My Spectrum," received critical acclaim for its honesty, humor, and heartfelt portrayal of Fern's journey.

Fern also continued to expand her literary work. She began writing a novel, drawing on her experiences and her vivid imagination to create a story that intertwined humor, life's complexities, and the nuances of being neurodiverse. The novel was eagerly anticipated by her fans, who had come to appreciate her unique voice and perspective in all her creative endeavors.

On the advocacy front, Fern was instrumental in launching a global initiative aimed at improving workplace inclusivity for neurodiverse individuals. Drawing from her own experiences in the entertainment industry, she worked with businesses and organizations to develop training programs and resources that fostered a more understanding and accommodating work environment for everyone.

Despite her growing list of accomplishments, Fern remained humble and approachable. She continued to engage with her fans and followers, sharing her life's ups and downs through her social media platforms. Her transparency and authenticity only endeared her more to the public, who saw in her not just a celebrity but a genuine, relatable individual.

As Fern approached the latter part of the decade, her influence as a comedian, writer, and advocate remained undiminished. Her work had touched countless lives, providing laughter, inspiration, and a sense of belonging to those who found themselves reflected in her stories and advocacy. Fern Marie Brady had become more than a name; she was a symbol of the beauty and strength found in embracing one's true self, and a reminder that everyone, regardless of their place on the spectrum of humanity, has a valuable story to tell. Her legacy continued to unfold, a testament to the enduring power of humor, empathy, and the human spirit.

As the decade turned, Fern Brady's influence as a cultural icon only continued to grow. The year 2030 marked a significant milestone in her career - the release of her much-anticipated novel, "The Spectrum Chronicles." The book was a triumphant blend of fiction and elements of memoir, weaving a narrative that was both deeply personal and universally resonant. Critics hailed it as a masterpiece of contemporary literature, praising its nuanced portrayal of neurodiversity and its rich, empathetic character development. Readers around the world found themselves deeply connected to the story, seeing reflections of their own lives in its pages.

This period also saw Fern branching out into new media. She began hosting a television show that blended comedy with serious discussions about mental health, neurodiversity, and social issues. The show, "Fern Brady's World," became a hit for its unique format and Fern's ability to engage with complex topics in an accessible, often humorous way. It not only entertained but also educated, shining a light on important issues that were often overlooked or misunderstood in mainstream media.

In her personal life, Fern maintained a strong connection to her Scottish roots. She purchased a small cottage in the Scottish Highlands, a tranquil retreat where she could write, reflect, and recharge away from the demands of her public life. This home became a sanctuary for her, surrounded by the rugged beauty of the landscape she loved so dearly.

Fern's advocacy work also took on a new dimension as she launched the "Brady Foundation for Neurodiversity." The foundation focused on supporting neurodiverse individuals in various aspects of life, from education and career development to mental health and community support. It quickly became a leading voice in the field, known for its impactful programs and its commitment to creating a more inclusive world.

Despite her many achievements, Fern remained grounded and focused on what truly mattered to her. She often spoke of the importance of staying true to oneself, of the value of kindness and compassion, and of the need to laugh even in the face of adversity. These messages resonated deeply with her audience, who saw her not just as a celebrity but as a wise and compassionate figure.

As Fern Brady looked towards the future, she continued to explore new creative avenues and ways to make a difference. Her journey was a testament to the power of resilience, the beauty of embracing one's unique identity, and the impact one person can have in making the world a more understanding and inclusive place. Her story, ever-evolving and rich with experience, remained an inspiration to countless individuals around the globe, a reminder that in our diversity lies our greatest strength.

As the 2030s progressed, Fern Brady's influence and creativity showed no signs of waning. She used her platform to tackle increasingly diverse and challenging topics, always with her trademark blend of humor and insight. Her voice became an anchor for many in a rapidly changing world, providing both solace and a sharp, critical perspective on contemporary issues.

In 2032, Fern embarked on a project that was close to her heart – a series of workshops and talks aimed at young people. Titled "Embrace Your Spectrum," these workshops focused on self-acceptance, mental health, and the power of storytelling. Fern traveled to schools and universities, sharing her experiences and encouraging young minds to find and use their unique voices. Her message was simple yet powerful: "Your differences are not just to be accepted; they are to be celebrated."

This initiative led to the publication of a children's book authored by Fern. The book, "The Adventures of Ellie the Elephant," was about a young, neurodiverse elephant who discovers her unique strengths through her adventures. Illustrated with vibrant colors and filled with charming characters, the book became a favorite among children and parents alike. It was praised for its positive representation of neurodiversity and its ability to discuss complex topics in a way that was accessible to young readers.

Fern's commitment to her roots in Scotland remained strong. She became involved in local community projects, particularly those focused on the arts and mental health. Her cottage in the Highlands turned into a creative hub, where artists, writers, and thinkers regularly gathered for retreats organized by Fern. These retreats became known for sparking creative collaborations and for being a breeding ground for innovative ideas.

In the mid-2030s, Fern surprised her fans by venturing into the world of theatre. She wrote and starred in a play that explored the life of a woman navigating the complexities of modern society as a neurodiverse individual. The play, titled "Uncharted Minds," received critical acclaim for its raw portrayal of life's challenges and triumphs, and for Fern's powerful performance. It toured major cities around the world, breaking box office records and leaving audiences deeply moved.

Throughout her career, Fern remained an outspoken advocate for mental health awareness and neurodiversity. She worked closely with various organizations to push for policy changes and better support systems for neurodiverse individuals. Her efforts were recognized globally, and she received numerous awards for her contributions to society.

As she approached her 50th birthday, Fern's legacy was firmly established. She was not just a comedian, writer, and advocate; she was a symbol of hope and resilience. Her journey had inspired a generation to embrace their identities, to find strength in their differences, and to approach life with humor and courage. Fern Brady's story was a beacon of light in a world that often struggled to understand the beauty of diversity. Her laughter, wisdom, and compassion continued to resonate, reminding everyone that in the rich tapestry of human experience, every thread, no matter how different, was essential and valuable.

As Fern Brady approached her 50s, her journey took a reflective turn. She began working on a new memoir, one that delved deeper into her experiences in the latter part of her career and her personal growth. The memoir, tentatively titled "Reflections in the Spectrum," was eagerly anticipated by her fans and critics alike. In it, Fern explored the nuances of aging, the evolving understanding of neurodiversity, and the ever-changing landscape of comedy and advocacy. Her writing was as sharp and witty as ever, but there was a new depth to it, a richness that came from years of experience and introspection.

Around this time, Fern also launched a new podcast series. Unlike her previous work, this podcast focused on intimate conversations with individuals from all walks of life, discussing their unique journeys and the lessons they learned along the way. The series, "Conversations on the Spectrum," quickly gained a following for its honest and heartfelt dialogue. It was a testament to Fern's skill as a communicator and her ability to connect with people on a deep level.

In her personal life, Fern found great joy in mentoring young comedians and writers, particularly those who were neurodiverse. She often spoke about the importance of passing on knowledge and opening doors for the next generation. Many of her mentees went on to have successful careers, and they frequently cited Fern's guidance and support as a key factor in their development.

Fern's influence in the realm of neurodiversity advocacy also continued to grow. She became a key figure in international conferences and symposiums, where she spoke about the importance of inclusive policies and practices. Her insights and recommendations were sought after by policymakers and educational institutions, leading to significant changes in how neurodiversity was approached in various sectors.

Despite her many commitments, Fern never lost her love for stand-up comedy. She continued to perform, albeit less frequently, bringing her unique brand of humor to audiences around the world. Her performances were special events, eagerly anticipated by her fans. On stage, Fern was in her element, her humor as incisive and relevant as ever, her connection with the audience palpable.

In the latter half of the 2030s, Fern began to focus on legacy projects. One such project was the establishment of the "Brady Centre for Neurodiversity and the Arts," a state-of-the-art facility that offered resources, training, and support for neurodiverse artists and performers. The center also hosted exhibitions, performances, and workshops, becoming a hub of creativity and inclusion.

As she reflected on her life and career, Fern often spoke about the journey of self-discovery and the unexpected paths life can take. Her story had become more than a tale of personal success; it was a narrative about the power of embracing one's true self, the importance of laughter and resilience, and the impact one individual can have in making the world a more understanding and compassionate place.

Fern Brady's legacy was not just in the laughter she brought to people's lives, or the changes she helped bring about in the understanding of neurodiversity. Her greatest legacy was in the countless individuals she inspired to live their lives authentically and courageously, to face challenges with humor and grace, and to make their own mark on the world in their unique ways. As Fern Brady continued her journey, her story remained a beacon of hope and a reminder that in the vibrant spectrum of humanity, every color has its place and its purpose.

Printed in the USA
CPSIA information can be obtained
at www.ICGtesting.com
LVHW010418110724
785188LV00003B/259